P9-DVT-700

ALSO BY STEPHEN R. COVEY & MANGO MEDIA

An Effective Life

The 7 Habits of Highly Effective People - Interactive Edition

The 7 Habits of Highly Effective People - Snapshots Edition

First Things First - Interactive Edition with A. Roger Merrill
and Rebecca R. Merrill

Great Work Great Career - Interactive Edition

Los 7 Hábitos de la Gente Altamente Efectiva: Edición de Imágenes

Copyright © 2016 by Franklin Covey.
Published by Mango Media Inc.

All icons and illustrations from www.shutterstock.com
and Franklin Covey.

All rights reserved. No part of this publication may be
reproduced, distributed or transmitted in any form or
by any means without prior written permission.

ISBN 978-1-63353-272-4

www.franklincovey.com

CONTENTS

INTRODUCTION

Stephen R. Covey was a master teacher.

Millions of people know this. It's not exactly a secret. But what people may not fully understand is that Stephen Covey was a master teacher because he was first a master student. He wasn't born Dr. Stephen R. Covey. As a little kid on the playground, he did not preach the principles of synergy during a particularly intense game of kickball. When he got older, he did not lecture visiting friends about putting first things first as they picked up toys before devouring an afternoon snack. It's an interesting idea. But it did not happen.

He paid attention to the world around him. He asked questions. He sought after new knowledge. And when he found a principle of knowledge that would help him be better, he fully embraced it. You can see this in *The 7 Habits of Highly Effective People*. People asked him all the time: "How? How did you come up with *The 7 Habits*?"

He would simply smile upon hearing the question, take a moment to contemplate it and then answer with impeccable timing: "I didn't." Of course, anyone asking the question was confused by this response. But before a follow-up question could be presented, he delivered the answer.

"I wrote the book," he would answer, "but the principles were known long before me. They are more like natural laws," he would say. "All I did was put them together to synthesize them for people."

Conversations were his classroom. When you met him, he would envelope you in his strong handshake, his inviting presence. Whether you were a family member, a close friend, or an acquaintance—even if you bumped into him casually—you could spend the next few hours engaged in a meaningful conversation about family, friends, work…life.

The principles he shared were timeless. He spent well over thirty years studying, practicing and refining the principles presented within *The 7 Habits of Highly Effective People*. He was always looking to teach these principles, to make them comprehendible and accomplishable.

Because he understood that never before has the world been so big. Opportunities unlike anything we have seen before await the next generation. But never before has the world been so small. Technology has linked us together in powerful and sometimes dangerous ways. The amount of knowledge at our fingertips is incalculable. With this grand amount of information, it becomes increasingly difficult to know what's right and what's wrong.

As you interact with the world, what questions do you ask? There are some basic ones that may come to mind such as: "Why is he driving so slowly in the left lane?"

That question seems to be asked a lot, especially in the morning and late afternoon. Naturally, a favorite question of parents tends to be: "What were you thinking?"

Those are not the questions we should dwell on, especially since the answers to those questions are never very good.

- What questions can you ask to keep learning?

- What knowledge can you gain by asking the right questions?

- What changes can you make by embracing the knowledge that you discover?

- What discipline is needed to make those changes a part of your true character?

There is no effectiveness without discipline and there is no discipline without character. And there is no character without first starting and asking questions.

Stephen R. Covey passed away in 2012. But he will never stop teaching. What you'll find on the following pages are a collection of his thoughts on topics that relate to living a Time Conscious Life.

He wholeheartedly believed that if everyone in the world lived by *The 7 Habits*, the world would be a better place. Jim Collins said a few years back that "no person lasts forever, but books and ideas can endure."

We hope that as you move forward through these pages, you will discover the message that goes beyond a simple lesson.

We hope that the message he crafted all those years ago continues to resonate with you and your friends and family.

--Stephen Covey's colleagues

THE BEGINNING

Time is an asset we all have in common and in an equal amount.

– Dr. Stephen R. Covey

Time can be a charitable and kind friend. Or conversely, Time can be the dreaded enemy knocking at the door.

Each and every day, Time doles out 24 hours to everyone. No matter the age, the level of wealth, or even the intended plans for those 24 hours, they are freely given.

Bonnie never saw Time as a friend. Time was something she fought against. Time was something she tried to wrestle and stretch. Time was something she tried every day to beat.

You see, Bonnie was busy. No one would dare dispute her stunning level of busyness. She wore her busyness as a proud badge of her personal worth. But at the end of the day, as she awaited her new 24 hours from Time, Bonnie would reflect on what she had done in the previous 24 hours.

"I know I was busy," she would think. "But what did I actually DO?"

As if it was a physical, stifling weight, Bonnie felt crushed by the guilt of what remained to be done or what could have been done. And she vowed to do a better job beating Time as she continued to tread through this state of busyness. She would force in even more busyness in her 24 hours.

Until another night came and Bonnie impatiently awaited her new 24 hours from Time. She reflected again on what had been done for the day.

"I know I was busy," she thought again. "But what did I actually DO?"

Bonnie felt defeated. She considered taking off her busyness badge from her image of self-worth but wondered what would take its place. If she was not busy, surely she was a failure.

A change was needed. When Time once again arrived and presented Bonnie with her 24 hours, Bonnie took a deep breath and asked:

"What can I do differently? What will I do with you today that will make a difference in how I spend my time?"

Bonnie's story is not an exclusive battle. Many people driving along the freeway of busyness and polishing that busyness badge to a perfect sheen have stopped, gotten off the road, and asked themselves: What can I do better?

There is no right answer to that question. The answer is as personal and unique as each individual. But an answer can nevertheless be found.

Stephen R. Covey promised: "You can lead your own life: an inspiring, trustworthy, contributing life."

But to lead your own life, you must first lead your time, your 24 hour days. Time makes up life. The two are inseparable.

Dr. Covey asked:

Are you ever too busy driving to take time to get gas? Too busy sawing to take time to sharpen the saw? We don't need more time. We have all the time there is. No one has more of it than anyone else. What we need to do is put priorities on our goals and activities and to manage ourselves accordingly, instead of allowing conditions to manage us. We always have time and take time for things which are really important to us.

Like Bonnie, you can take your gift from Time and ask:

What will I do with you today that will make a difference in how I spend my time?

And then a miracle can happen. You can develop a time-conscious life dedicated to taking:

- Time to Live;

- Time to Love;

- Time to Learn; and

- Time to Leave a Legacy.

This book is not designed to be simply read; it's designed to be experienced.

The message is powerful, practical, and immediately applicable and communicated through quotes, experiences and infographics.

At the end of this book, you will find the Personal Journal: Experiencing a More Time Conscious Life. If you wish to incorporate what you read, the personal journal can help. By asking introspective questions, we hope to provide you with a tool to carve out a road to reach that desired change. Please take advantage of every single page.

This book is designed to help readers on the path to a more time conscious life. Walk with us.

CHAPTER 1
Live

YOUR UNIQUE TALENTS AND CAPABILITIES
DETERMINE THE IMPORTANT WORK YOU HAVE
TO DO IN LIFE.

The tragedy is that our unique contribution is often never made because the important "first things" in our lives are choked out by other urgent things.

And so some important works are never started or finished.

My good friend, Alan O'Neill, once told me about the 10 minute journey. This time conscious philosophy is one that I would like to share with you.

A few years back, Alan was feeling really disconnected. He got into meditation and other things to help him get rid of the rapid head talk and connect with who he was from the inside. But quite frankly, despite his intentions and best efforts, he was having difficulty making that connection. So he prepared himself to take a three-day vision quest on a mountain. He planned to fast. He carried water, a sleeping bag, and a journal—and that was it. Only 10 minutes into the journey, he had his first lesson. He heard a rattle and saw a snake strike at his walking stick about six inches from his foot.

For a moment, fear overwhelmed him. But then he remembered that everything on this journey was supposed to be a lesson for his understanding and growth, so he tried to step back from his fear and learn. The snake curled up on a large boulder that was close to him.

As he stood still and looked at it, he had a sudden, powerful paradigm shift. It was almost as if he established instant communication with that snake, and he felt overwhelmed with what he was experiencing. No longer was the snake something to be feared. He saw its oneness with nature. He saw the beauty in it, and started thinking, **"If I can accept the beauty in this snake, what is it within my own being that I am fearing and not accepting?"**

He also recognized that all things are equal in creation, and that the fear of the unknown leads to prejudgment of things that are different. He began to better understand the issue of wholeness, the connection of everything to the divine.

The anecdote with the snake has taught me not to fear. Where before I, like you, had a lot of well-masked fear—about everything from speaking in front of a group to dealing with upset stakeholders or people who relied on power and control—I can honestly say now that there's really nothing that I am fearful of in the work environment.

My response is totally different.

That day, the snake was not the only encounter to teach Alan and us.

The sunset he saw at the end taught him to open up to others. And if we open up, others are willing to open up, too, and it really makes a difference in how we operate.

I've found that sometimes you just have to be vulnerable and not worry about whether people will think you're crazy or not.

Nature and time are constantly teaching us. A storm teaches us to be calm in the midst of other storms. The ladybugs help us learn that everyone is special, that everyone's role is important. The snakes, the sunset, the storm and the ladybug, they all have their respective roles, and more importantly, their time to shine.

I believe that character, what a person is, is ultimately more important than competence, what a person can do.

Obviously both are important, but **character is foundational**. All else builds on this cornerstone.

Even the very best structure, system, style, and skills can't compensate completely for deficiencies in character.

Until you choose your own
motives, you really **can't**
choose to live
YOUR OWN LIFE.
Everything flows out of
MOTIVE AND MOTIVATION
—that is the root of
OUR DEEPEST DESIRES.

We all live three lives: public, private, and secret.

In our public lives, we are seen and heard by colleagues, associates, and others within our circle of influence.

In our private lives, we interact more intimately with spouses, family members, and close friends.

The secret life is part of the other two.

The secret life is where your heart is, where your real motives are—the ultimate desires of your life.

Proactivity means more than merely taking initiative. **It means that we are responsible for our own lives.**

We recognize that *responsibility* means the ability to choose our response. We do not blame circumstances, conditions, or conditioning for our behavior.

Our behavior is a product of our choices, based on principles, rather than a product of our conditions, based on feelings.

If people live out of their memory, they're bound to the past; if they live out of **IMAGINATION**, they create opportunity.

Most people live with the lie that they can get away with doing unwise things in private or in secret—that it won't affect their work or family.

That's living a lie.

It gets translated in a thousand and one different ways.

I find the following three practices to be very helpful in the process of self-affirmation.

Use relaxation techniques to plant affirmations.
Affirmations can achieve effective results in the rush of everyday living. The mind and the body must slow down.

Use repetition to ensure success. If you desire to use your affirmation to initiate change or to prepare yourself for some future event, you must experience it over and over. Say it, see it, feel it. Make it a part of you. Instead of living the scripts given by your parents, your friends, society, or the environment, you're affirming, you're living the new scripts given by your own self-discovered value system.

Use imagination and visualization to see the change. In any affirmation, the more details you can see in your mind's eye, and the more clear and vivid the details—the color, the texture, the smells, the sounds, the time, the place—the less you will view your affirmation as a spectator and the more you will experience it as a participant. Most of us grossly neglect this creative power. We live too much out of our memories, too little out of our imaginations.

Begin to work on improvement. Appraise your situation and analyze it.

Why do we behave as we do?

Strive for objectivity by analyzing what happens in our relationships with other people.

Are we effective?

Are we ineffective?

We then plan and take positive action.

After the positive action, mentally reflect upon it. Plan and then act again. Reflect again.

This constant educational process will enable you to talk intelligently with yourself, communicate with yourself, and to understand and accept yourself.

While we must learn from good examples and always keep in mind **THE BIGGER GOAL,** We must compare ourselves **ONLY WITH OUR SELF.** We can't focus or base our happiness on another's progress; we can focus **ONLY ON OUR OWN.**

We need a sense of self-esteem, this feeling that we are true to ourselves, that we are good apart from our performance or our particular point of view.

Photographer Dewitt Jones helped me understand how perspective and time go hand-in-hand.

What perspective will you use to view the problem in order to find a creative solution? If I don't have the right perspective going in, I don't have a chance of finding the extraordinary view.

I use that metaphor Dewitt taught in the rest of my life as well. I'm always asking myself in my business or in my relationship with my community or my family, **"Do I have the right perspective? Do I have the right point of view?"**

CHAPTER 2

Love

As we treat one another with more

LOVE, KINDNESS, COURTESY, HUMILITY, PATIENCE, AND FORGIVENESS

we encourage the same in return.

Our relationship with ourselves affects and is influenced by our relationships with others; conversely, our relationship with others is based on our relationship with ourselves.

Our ability to get along well with others flows naturally from how well we get along with ourselves, from our own internal peace and harmony.

To get closer to partners or customers, for example, we

may need to make some changes in our own attitudes and behaviors.

When I like and respect myself more, I find it easier to like and respect others more.

I give more freely of myself. I'm less defensive and guarded, more open and respectful of others.

Parents should be very wise and see any situation as it really is and not overreact or give up on themselves, but simply hang in there, rolling with the punches, smiling a lot, loving unconditionally.

They should write these affirmations on walls, mirrors, forearms, and hearts:

"Steady as she goes."

"This, too, shall pass."

"Don't take it personally."

"Roll with the punches."

They will find that if they continuously reaffirm and hold steady and consistent, true and faithful, if they model true interdependence with each family member and **truly love unconditionally**, then each family member **will know where the unconditional love supply is.**

WE CAN LEARN
NOT TO BE OFFENDED.

We can cultivate our security from
within, based on integrity to
fundamental principles, so that we can
LOVE
when we're not loved,
be KIND
when people aren't kind to us, and
PATIENT
when they're impatient with us.

OUR ROLE IN RELATIONSHIPS IS TO BE A
LIGHT, NOT A JUDGE.

We hear a great deal on how to overcome insecurity and inferiority and how to acquire confidence and inner peace. But few advice-givers work on the roots of the human soul and the laws and plan of life. Self-alienation is the root cause of relationship breakdowns.

Synergy is creatively producing better solutions than what we had before.

This requires deep empathic listening and great courage in expressing perspectives and opinions in ways that show respect for the other person's view.

Out of that genuine interaction come insights and learnings that are truly synergistic.

Synergy can't be forced or manipulated. It has to come naturally from the quality of the relationship—the friendship, trust, and love that unites people.

The lesson again for us as students of human relations is to attempt to develop this quality we call empathy. That is the ability to see the world as others see it, to cease judging and work from an accepting position.

This creates the atmosphere in which others will listen to constructive criticism, in which they will begin to grow and develop.

The great barrier to communication is the tendency to constantly evaluate or moralize with others.

The great gateway to this communication process is to learn to listen and to listen intentively and with understanding, to listen acceptingly to the other fellow's point of view. This then creates an atmosphere of love and approval.

Valuing the individual, particularly the unlovable, the obnoxious, the awkward, the 'drop out', communicates powerfully and persuasively to all the rest, your sincere regard and loving concern for them as individuals.

WE ALL NEED LOVE, UNDERSTANDING,
AND ACCEPTANCE.

To merely be with a person and spend time with him communicates intrinsic value.

Your child knows from watching you all day how much you value time.

To listen, to attempt to understand, to be patient, and kind, and considerate takes time.

Thus, you communicate that **you value him** intrinsically.

INTELLIGENT RELATIONSHIPS
MUST BE BASED UPON
PLANNING AND PREPARATION.

We cannot blunder into other people's presence, particularly where bad feelings exist, and expect to enjoy peace and good communication.

TO CAREFULLY LISTEN IS A
POWERFUL WAY OF SAYING
TO ANOTHER THAT WE VALUE HIM.

When we take the time to understand and stay with it until the other feels that we do understand, we have communicated many things:

- we care,

- we want to understand,

- we respect their expression,

and we give them dignity and an individual sense of worth.

The only real way to build a relationship or to strengthen a relationship that has been strained is on a one-to-one basis—to go to that person to make reconciliation, to talk the matter over, to apologize, to forgive, or whatever it might take.

If you can love—deeply, richly—in affirming another person, you will help him **TO CHANGE, TO DEVELOP, TO GROW.** It is almost ironic because some people think that if you do that, you make the other person become complacent and stultified. **I believe that the very opposite results.**

A basic need which resides in all of us is a social need—to have a sense of belonging, to have opportunity to express friendship and love, and to receive friendship and love; to have an association with other people and to feel an acceptance socially.

We enjoy these interrelationships. We enjoy the opportunity
to have an increasing number of them.

I suggest that we attempt in all our relationships with other people to establish a climate of approval and of **acceptance of people as they are** so that they do not have to pretend in our presence to be someone whom they are not.

**AS LEADERS WE
CAN SET THE TONE**

By courageously accepting ourselves, we accept and love others which helps them to
ACCEPT THEMSELVES
and such an attitude can disseminate itself down through our entire organization to its everlasting betterment. This is why love is the greatest thing in the world—and why it is the heart and soul of
EFFECTIVE LEADERSHIP.

CHAPTER 3

Learn

Ongoing study and learning will prepare you for future opportunity.

Continuous learning will keep you in control, even with all the changes in the economy.

But if you stop learning, especially in areas vital to your career path, you will soon be obsolete.

People must accept the personal responsibility to upgrade their knowledge and skills, to become computer literate or gain advanced computer literacy, to read widely, and to be aware of the powerful forces that are operating in their environments.

They may need to gain or regain a liberal and fine arts education, in addition to keeping up on what is happening in the world of technology and science, because the arts and sciences create the capacity of the mind to keep learning.

When we talk about learning and increasing our capacities and competencies, we usually think in terms of technical competence or conceptual competence.

We rarely think in terms of a social competence that seeks a mutual win or in terms of character. And yet, ultimately, if a person is to bring about meaningful, lasting change or significant improvement, that person will need to cultivate the characteristics of interdependency, empathy and synergy as well as the qualities of integrity, maturity, and the abundance mentality.

I would argue that separate and apart from our jobs, we all have a moral obligation

TO LEARN AND PROGRESS.

And lifelong learning is not so much about big campaigns and programs, academic degrees and credentials, as it is about short daily study sessions and small doses of relevant on-the-job training.

THE PRINCIPLE OF BALANCE IS KEY TO CONTINUOUS LEARNING.

I recommend a balance between personal and organizational development; between current job-related needs and future requirements; between industry-related learning and general education.

Make sure that your approach is systematic and based on feedback to you personally and professionally.

Your learning should balance theory with practice, arts with the sciences.

MAKE SURE THAT YOUR LEARNING AND
DEVELOPMENT ARE MOTIVATED BY A DESIRE
TO BE OF GREATER SERVICE.

Unless people learn, change, grow, and progress to accommodate the market, there can be no security.

SECURITY LIES IN THE POWER
TO CONTINUALLY LEARN.

The best way to learn something is
TO TEACH IT.
Now, most people already know the truth of this principle. It is almost self-evident. Still, it is not used much in business, or even in education. And yet the single most important thing I have learned in the field of training and development is to
TEACH WHAT YOU LEARN
to others.

I have frequently counseled people who wanted better jobs to show more initiative—to take interest and aptitude tests, to study the industry, even specific problems the organizations they are interested in are facing—and then to develop an effective presentation showing how their abilities can help solve these problems.

I call it "solution selling," and it's a key to business success. Many people wait for something to happen or someone to take care of them. But people who land the best jobs are solutions to problems, not problems themselves. They seize the initiative to do whatever is necessary, consistent with correct principles, to get the job done.

You need to learn new skills to nurture relationships that have real endurance and have their own immune system-relationships that are based on empathic consideration and courageous expression, as well as on synergy-seeking a transcendent purpose that enables you to get away from positional bargaining and politics.

Inquisitiveness is the essence of global leadership because it makes you want to learn since it helps you recognize how much you don't know.

AS A SIDE BENEFIT, LEARNING LANGUAGES, CULTURES, CUSTOMS, AND DIFFERENT BEST PRACTICES KEEPS YOU HUMBLE AND TEACHABLE.

To be humble and constantly learning is good, regardless of
the reason.

WE ALL NEED TO BEGIN TO IMPROVE,
STARTING FROM WHERE WE ARE, NOT
FROM WHERE WE SHOULD BE, OR WHERE
SOMEONE ELSE IS, OR EVEN FROM WHERE
OTHERS MAY THINK WE ARE.

By doing one more pushup each day, I could do 30 in a month.

Likewise, in any area of improvement, I could also exercise a little more of what it takes, such as:

- a little more patience,

- a little more understanding,

- a little more moral courage,

thus slowly increasing my capacity through daily effort and discipline.

Even though every job has its monotonous, challenging aspects, all of us have abundant opportunity somewhere, sometime in our lives to expand our interests, deepen our knowledge and develop our skills and our abilities to participate actively in and to promote those interests— in short, **to become involved in life.**

Is the gaining of knowledge the main purpose of continued education?

I don't believe so.

The knowledge explosion is so vast and so rapid, no one, giving all his time, could keep up.

If it's not knowledge, what then is it?

To keep intellectually alive, to renew ourselves, to learn how to learn, how to adapt, how to change, and what not to change.

UNLESS WE ACCEPT OURSELVES where we are, we cannot then begin to progress. The beginning of education, therefore, is the **REALIZATION OF IGNORANCE.**

When we feel accepted and loved as we are, our defenses are relaxed and we become susceptible and ready for learning, for insight, for critical examination, for change and development.

CHAPTER 4

Leave A Legacy

THE BEST WAY TO PREDICT YOUR FUTURE
IS TO CREATE IT.

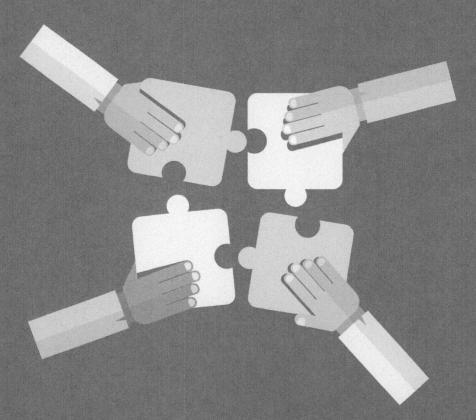

The key to happiness is to live outside yourself—to **WORK TOGETHER WITH OTHERS** in love for a common vision or mission that gives meaning.

I have learned that few great plans are finished in one lifetime, and that our service and contribution may well represent the continuation of an intergenerational vision.

THE BEST WAY TO CHANGE THE WORLD
IS TO CHANGE YOUR HEAD, THAT IS, YOUR
THINKING, YOUR PERCEPTIONS.

Remember, you see the world as you are, not as it is.
You are the map of your world.

What a person is teaches far more eloquently than what a person says or even does.

It communicates quietly, subtly; it is a constant radiation, and others, though unable to identify it or articulate it, still understand it, sense it, absorb it, and respond to it.

People who neglect their families to climb that proverbial ladder of success often learn too late that the ladder is leaning against the wrong wall. **NO ONE**, on their deathbed, ever wished they'd spent **MORE TIME AT THE OFFICE.** People who come to our leadership workshops, primarily to help their businesses, return home with a much **STRONGER FOCUS ON FAMILY.**

THE HIGHEST FORM OF INFLUENCE IS TO
BE A MODEL, NOT A CRITIC; A LIGHT, NOT
A JUDGE.

There are specific things parents can do to teach

RESPONSIBILITY, RESPECT, VIRTUE, OBEDIENCE, WORK,

and other principles.

But first they must really commit themselves to parenthood responsibility as their highest priority, and must be willing to give their best time, their best thinking, their highest loyalty and enthusiasm and dedication to this task.

As with other things, there is no shortcut to this process of character development. There is only one law that governs—the law of the harvest.

WE WILL REAP WHAT WE SOW.

YOU TEACH WHAT YOU ARE.

We will approach our secular work with careful planning, using the best systems, keeping careful records, spending time to analyze the problems; but with the character development of our own children we often go on day-in and day-out without any real analysis or planning or record keeping, without any intelligent system.

THE ENEMY OF THE BEST
IS OFTEN THE GOOD.

The capacity to turn the other cheek, go the extra mile, and be a servant leader comes from a deep vision of what we're trying to accomplish.

WE SEE WHAT WE SEEK.

If we seek a great thing, we tend to see greatness inside people if they're part of it.

And we seek feedback from people who have the courage to share.

We're not killing the messenger who brings us feedback. Rather, we show appreciation and have the humility to apologize and say, "I need to improve and make amends."

HOW AM I GOING TO ACT?

I read an editorial in the newspaper the other day to this effect: A Quaker friend and I walked up to the newsstand and bought a newspaper.

And then thanked the newspaper man politely. The newsman answered nothing.

"A sullen fellow, isn't he?" I commented.

"Yes, he's that way every night," my friend answered.

"Well then, why do you continue to be so polite and nice to him?" I asked.

"Why not?" he answered me. "Why should I let him decide how I am going to act?"

The crucial element in this man's life was that he had sufficient internal security within himself that he did not depend upon the attitude of others to affect his attitude.

If we believe in the human dignity concept, and have faith in it and act on it, we will release enormous energies in people toward the fulfillment of great things.

To me this is our challenge, our great problem, and I wish us all success as we work on it.

THE RUNNING CLOCK

Hazel O'Leary, the Chairman of Keystone Energy Group, and the former U.S. Secretary of Energy, shared a story with me about the Running Clock that might bring tears to your eyes.

More than a decade ago her husband, Jack, died suddenly. He had been vigorous physically, mentally, and spiritually.

Neither she nor the rest of the family were prepared for his death, and they had difficulty reconciling themselves to the loss.

Just prior to his death, they had built a new home. The landscape design was planned as a joint project, and now the plan had to be implemented without him. Clearing, planting, and cultivating had to be done in every corner of the property.

My friend dug into the earth and ripped out debris with a passion. She planted and watered. And little by little, she found herself healing.

By the time the plants and flowers started to grow, she was watching them with almost a fascination. She realized that they were teaching her about life and death, about growth and rebirth, about the Running Clock. She came to understand that life is a cycle, and that death is an important part of that cycle.

In your mind's eye, picture your 80th birthday.

Picture the faces of the people there, the faces of your friends and family as they come to wish you well. Laughter and smiles surround a full dining table as the people you love the most enjoy the night.

All these people have come to honor you, to express their feelings, and to toast a life well spent. Imagine you are the person being honored, the subject of the speeches.

What would you like the speakers to say about you, and your life?

What would you like them to say about your character and contributions?

Now think deeply, what achievements you would want them to remember. What impact would you have liked to have made in their lives?

Start living today with that picture of your own 80th birthday party clearly in mind. In that picture you will find your definition of true success.

What type of legacy would you like to leave?

A MASTERPIECE

If life was a painting, and you were the artist, what would you paint?

Would you paint a portrait of yourself?

Perhaps a portrait of your true love?

How would you paint your most passionate hopes?

When others see your painting, what will they remember?

THIS IS YOUR LIFE, MAKE IT A MASTERPIECE.

I invite you to search your own heart as you ask yourself this question:

What legacy will I leave?

Such searching often stirs up reinvention, redesign, and restructuring because you realize that you must pay the price for profitable growth.

STEPHEN R. COVEY was an internationally respected leadership authority, family expert, teacher, organizational consultant, and author who dedicated his life to teaching principle-centered living and leadership to build both families and organizations. He earned an M.B.A. from Harvard University and a doctorate from Brigham Young University, where he was a professor of organizational behavior and business management and also served as director of university relations and assistant to the president.

Dr. Covey was the author of several acclaimed books, including the international bestseller, *The 7 Habits of Highly Effective People*, which was named the #1 Most Influential Business Book of the Twentieth Century and one of the top-ten most influential management books ever. It has sold more than 25 million copies in more than 40 languages throughout the world. Other bestsellers include *First Things First, Principle-Centered Leadership, The 7 Habits of Highly Effective Families, The 8th Habit,* and *The 3rd Alternative* bringing the combined total to more than 30 million books sold.

As a father of nine and grandfather of forty-three, he received the 2003 Fatherhood Award from the National Fatherhood Initiative, which he said was the most meaningful award he ever received.

Other awards given to Dr. Covey include the Thomas More College Medallion for continuing service to humanity, Speaker of the Year in 1999, the Sikh's 1998 International Man of Peace Award, the 1994 International Entrepreneur of the Year Award, and the National Entrepreneur of the Year Lifetime Achievement Award for Entrepreneurial Leadership. Dr. Covey was recognized as one of Time magazine's 25 Most Influential Americans and received seven honorary doctorate degrees.

Dr. Covey was the cofounder and vice chairman of FranklinCovey Co., the leading global professional services firm, with offices in more than 140 countries. FranklinCovey shares Dr. Covey's vision, discipline, and passion to inspire, lift, and provide tools for change and growth.

PERSONAL JOURNAL

Experiencing a Time Conscious Life

At the beginning of this book, the challenge was presented to move beyond simply reading this book. It's designed to be experienced.

To stop driving along the freeway of busyness and polishing that busyness badge to a perfect sheen. To stop and consider: What can I do better?

And now you're here. This is exactly where you can begin to embrace the quotes presented by Dr. Stephen R. Covey.

As you've read the messages, some ideas may have been sparked.

The purpose of this journal is to not lose those ideas—to not lose those sparks—but turn them into a roaring fire.

This Personal Journal will require work.

Did we lose you?

It's not mind-numbing work. It's not stressful work. It's not even tedious work.

But as you work through this journal, it could spark a change. It could change everything.

As previously stated, even a miracle can happen. You can develop a time conscious life dedicated to taking:

• Time to Live;

• Time to Love;

• Time to Learn; and

• Time to Leave a Legacy.

Each theme will have questions in this Personal Journal.

We've provided space for you to respond to each question, but feel free to write your answers in a private notebook that may provide you with a greater opportunity to expound on your ideas and fan those sparks.

Are you ready? Great! Because so are we!

LIVE

What is the important work only you can do? Do you give
this work enough time and attention? If not, what should
you change to ensure it does not get choked out?

LIVE

If character is your foundation, how satisfied are you with your personal foundation? What principles or materials are part of your foundation that make you proud? Are there any cracks you would like to repair? If yes, what are they and what is your plan?

LIVE

Can you think of a time this week when you were proactive? How did it change your week? What other areas of your life could benefit from being as proactive? What's your plan?

LIVE

Explain how it can be harmful to compare yourself to others.

LIVE

Reflect on this quote by Dr. Covey:

"We need a sense of self-esteem, this feeling that we are true to ourselves, that we are good apart from our performance on our particular point of view."

Describe where you are in the process of developing this self-esteem.

LOVE

Consider the quote by Dr. Covey:

"Our ability to get along well with others flows naturally from how well we get along with ourselves, from our own internal peace and harmony."

What is your personal dialogue? How can you improve it? In what ways can you be kinder to yourself?

LOVE

Who loves you unconditionally? How does that make you feel? Name one person you love unconditionally. Write about your feelings for this person. Is there someone in your life that could benefit from your unconditional love?

LOVE

Describe a situation where you were offended. Think about your reaction and the consequences. Can you describe how the situation could have been different? Is there an action that you could have been taken to produce a better outcome?

LOVE

Is listening one of your strengths? Write about a time when you were able to listen with empathy. Write about a time when someone listened to you with empathy. How did both experiences affect your relationship with that person?

LOVE

Consider the relationships that absorb the greatest amount of your time. Are your most valued relationships receiving your best time? What are you doing right? What do you plan to do better?

LEARN

Describe how you are continually learning. What are you doing well? What would you like to do next?

LEARN

Is your learning balanced?
Explain how you balance personal with professional learning.
If you don't feel there is balance, what can you change?

LEARN

Consider the following quote by Dr. Covey:

"Make sure that your learning and development are motivated by a desire to be of greater service."

Explain why that particular motivation is important.

LEARN

Dr. Covey stated that learning can help people become humble and teachable. But the exact opposite can also occur.

What do you believe makes the difference?

LEARN

If the best way to learn is to teach, how can you find more opportunities to teach in your profession? In your community? In your home?

LEAVE A LEGACY

What will be your greatest contribution?

LEAVE A LEGACY

What do you believe it means to have your ladder leaning against the wrong wall?   Have you recently moved your ladder? Or do you need to move your ladder? Why?

LEAVE A LEGACY

Describe how you can be a light, and not a judge in your profession, community, and home.

LEAVE A LEGACY

What thoughts came to mind when you read the story of
the 80th Birthday Celebration? Write answers to each of the
questions posed in the story.

LEAVE A LEGACY

Consider the visual image created by comparing your life to a painting. What are you painting? Outline the steps you are taking, or would like to take, to create a masterpiece.

CPSIA information can be obtained
at www.ICGtesting.com
Printed in the USA
LVOW01s2302221215
467488LV00001BA/1/P